Democracy in the United Kin

C000135810

Possible alternatives for the governance of Scotland

Background and current status of the governance of Scotland.

The Scottish devolution referendum of 1997 result demonstrated a clear desire of the people of Scotland to have their own parliament. The referendum questions not only asked the voters if they wanted a devolved Scottish Parliament but if such a parliament should have tax-varying powers. The majority of the electorate voted "Yes" to both proposals and the UK Parliament subsequently passed the Scotland Act in 1998 establishing for the first time since 1235 (ended by the Act of Union in 1707), a Scottish Parliament.

The Scottish Parliament currently enjoys devolved powers that have been transferred from the Parliament in Westminster. The Scottish Parliament in Holyrood, Edinburgh can pass laws on matters such as housing, culture, sport and the arts, education and training, agriculture, forestry and fisheries, health and social services, law and order, fire services, health and social services, social work, local government, environment and planning, tourism and economic development and many aspects of transport. It cannot make laws on reserved matters – these are matters that have a UK-wide or international dimension, such as immigration, defence and nuclear energy.

In 2012 following the recommendations of the Calman Commission, the Scotland Act was amended to give more powers to the Scottish Parliament. These new powers included:

- a new Scottish rate of income tax (from April 2016). The UK Government will deduct 10p in the £ from basic, higher and additional rates of income tax and the Scottish Parliament will have the power to levy a Scottish rate across these three bands.
- new borrowing powers for the Scottish Government
- full control of stamp duty land tax and landfill tax (from April 2015)
- the power to introduce new taxes, subject to agreement of the UK Government
- the power to make laws on matters relating to air weapons
- powers relating to the misuse of drugs, the drink-drive limit, the national speed limit and the administration of elections to the Scottish Parliament.

The Scotland Act of 2016 devolved even further powers to the Scottish Parliament. Recommendations were made by the Smith Commission in 2014 in the aftermath of the Scottish independence referendum of the same year. The additional law-making powers included:

- Abortion
- Consumer advocacy and advice
- Equal opportunities
- Gaming machines
- Parking
- Policing of railways in Scotland
- Speed limits
- Traffic signs

Alternative status for the governance of Scotland: Scottish Independence

In September 2014 the Scottish electorate was asked "Should Scotland be an independent country?" The franchise was extended to include 16 and 17 year olds; turnout was 84.6% and the 55% voted to remain part of the UK.

The arguments for Scottish independence were centred on taking back control of Scotland for the benefit of the people for Scotland and the nation's future. It is argued that an independent Scotland would encourage fairness and enable the people of Scotland to elect a government that represents them. The Scottish government is currently led by the Scottish National Party.

The SNP has long supported the political vision of a Scotland that is independent of the UK Government. The SNP believe that "to be in the driving seat of our own destiny and to shape our own future is a natural desire". A recent poll in Scotland revealed between 48% and 52% of people in Scotland support independence. It may be the case that the Brexit result has confirmed some people's desire to seek independence and even swayed "No" voters to "Yes" for Scottish independence.

The SNP is keen to protect the powers that have been devolved to the Scottish Parliament, such as healthcare, in the wake of the UK's departure from the EU. The SNP report that the UK government could open the NHS up to privatisation to get a trade deal with the United States – and the Scottish Parliament could have no say at all.

The Scottish Government and Holyrood's Finance & Constitution Committee agree that the UK Withdrawal Bill, as currently drafted, is not compatible with devolution. To ensure that Scotland's laws do not stop working properly on the day the UK leaves the EU, the Scottish Government has introduced a Scottish EU Continuity Bill. The Scottish EU Continuity Bill will ensure that there is no disruption to Scotland's laws after Brexit.

This is significant as it shows that in the wake of Brexit, the case for seeking independence for Scotland has strengthened. The SNP website states that the UK government may use Brexit as a means of grabbing power back from Scotland and so claims that "...this Bill safeguards Holyrood's devolved powers – rather than subject them to Westminster Tory diktat."

It would also be the case that an independent Scotland, with an SNP government, would have the power to remove the nuclear weapons currently stationed at the Clyde Naval Base. Known as 'Trident', the UK maintains four Vanguard-class submarines armed with Trident II D-5 ballistic missiles, able to deliver thermonuclear warheads from multiple independently targetable re-entry vehicles (MIRVs). Each submarine carries up to eight missiles and forty warheads.

One submarine is always on patrol. Anti-nuclear campaigners do not support the stockpiling or presence of nuclear weapons while the SNP state that "It's wrong – strategically, morally and financially".

There is widespread opposition to the renewal of Trident which is costly. Extending the life of the current Trident missiles into the early 2060s will cost around £250 million. Keeping the current Trident submarines in operation until 2028, four years longer than planned, is also expected to cost between £1.2 and £1.4 billion.

Despite SNP opposition, the Party claims that, "Westminster has written a blank cheque to base another generation of nuclear weapons in Scotland's waters". On 19 July 2016, 58 of Scotland's 59 MPs voted against the decision to renew the Trident nuclear weapons system.

This is important as it shows that there is a strong desire in Scotland to make decisions about Scotland's future in terms of defence and public spending. Independence would offer an alternative approach for the governance of Scotland which many people feel would be fairer and more representative of the wishes of the Scottish people and political representatives.

The SNP claims that most countries are now "nuclear-fee" and Trident does not address growing modern threats such as cyberattacks and terrorism. It could be argued that when Trident was created at the height of the Cold War, a nuclear deterrent was necessary, however this threat has now passed and so Trident is obsolete.

It could be argued that the current governance of Scotland allows for the nation to enjoy far-reaching benefits of autonomy with regards significant issues that affect directly the lives of the people of Scotland. That said, in the light of the UK's decision to leave the European Union, SNP MSPs are calling for further extensions to these devolved powers. Critics of the current status of Scotland's governance point to the result of the Brexit referendum in Scotland where almost two-thirds (62%) of the Scottish electorate voted to remain in the EU. First Minister, Nicola Sturgeon commented on ITV's Peston on Sunday television programme in May 2018 that:

"Once we get some clarity...about the Brexit outcome and the future relationship between the UK and the EU, then I will consider again the question of the timing of an independence referendum."

Critics of Brexit and limited devolution believe that there is a democratic deficit in Scotland as a result of the decision to leave the EU. Critics believe that since Scotland remains part of the UK, but the majority of the electorate in Scotland do not wish to leave the EU, Scotland should seek independence and try to gain membership of the EU alone. They feel that their political wishes are not being represented adequately and therefore feel that the time to try for a second Scottish independence referendum has arrived.

When the UK leaves the EU, the provisions of the Scotland Act 1998 limiting the power of the Scottish Parliament and

Government to make law and perform executive functions respectively, would be difficult if not impossible in some areas. The UK government has been accused of trying to grab power from the devolved assemblies. The UK government claims that control of some devolved matters such as agriculture and fishing, is temporary and will ensure a smooth transition of the transfer of power from Brussels to the UK.

When the EU Withdrawal Bill was debated in June 2018, MPs spent less than 20 minutes discussing the Bill's impact on devolution. The SNP said that showed "contempt for Scottish democracy", with the party's Westminster leader, Ian Blackford, leading a walk-out of his MPs during Prime Minister's Questions. This has led to a break-down in political relations between the Prime Minister, Theresa May and First Minister, Nicola Sturgeon.

Alternative status for the governance of Scotland: Devo-Max (Full fiscal autonomy)

Dev-max – also known as maximum devolution - would give Holyrood the power over most reserved matters, except defence and foreign affairs. Scotland would enjoy the extension of its devolved powers and this would include:

- The constitution
- Economic policy
- Public expenditure
- Benefits
- International relations
- Defence
- Immigration and nationality
- Access to information
- Business law
- Labour market law
- Consumer protection
- Energy
- Transport
- Broadcasting

It means Scotland would be 100% reliant on its own economy to pay for its services. It is possible that, unlike independence, devo-max could gain cross-party support in the Scottish Parliament because it does not threaten the union between Scotland and the rest of the UK.

Devo-max feels to many as the best of both worlds – Scotland would not be impacted by a potential change in currency, its devolved powers would not only be protected, but extended. It is not hard to envisage a situation where a Devo Max Scotland could transition very easily into independence so for many supporters of an independent Scotland, devo-max could offer a helpful stepping stone to an inevitable separation from the UK.

A Panelbase survey carried out in 2014 found that devo max had majority backing from supporters of all parties, with 59% of those who voted Liberal Democrat in the 2011 Scottish election in favour, 60% of Tory voters, 62% of Labour voters, 71% of Green voters and 79% of SNP voters. It was backed by 71% of men, 62% of women, all age groups and all socio-economic classes. This is significant as it reveals that devo-max appears to be a popular alternative for the governance of Scotland. Unlike independence, which is an emotive, sensitive and permanent separation of Scotland from the UK, devo-max could offer the people of Scotland greater powers without a permanent separation. As a result, devo-max feels less 'risky' to some and therefore a viable alternative for the governance of Scotland.

For some, devo-max does not go far enough as an alternative form of governance for Scotland. Blair Jenkins, Chief Executive of "Yes Scotland", said in 2014 that "independence was the only way to guarantee more powers for Holyrood". That said, critics of devo-max claim that while this extension of powers seems attractive and offers fairer representation, the associated costs would be astronomical for the Scottish government and this would impact directly and negatively the people of Scotland who would likely experience a decrease in government spending on healthcare and education, and an increase in income tax. All taxes would be levied and collected in Scotland, with a small sum then being paid by the Scottish government back to Westminster for shared services.

This would mean that Scotland would have full fiscal autonomy – full control of its finances and economy. This would mean that the Scottish government could set taxes and benefits at a level it feels would benefit the people of Scotland. It would be inevitable that income tax would increase, and while this action would be unpopular with some, others may consider that higher taxes, particularly for those on high incomes, are necessary for the greater good of Scotland as this would provide more money for public resources, such as hospitals.

Higher taxes for individuals and businesses operating in Scotland may result in a decline in investment and workers being dissuaded from moving to Scotland as they may feel that they will be impacted negatively when it comes to the amount of money they take home after paying income tax that is higher than the rest of the UK. This could prove to be damaging to the Scottish economy and therefore devo-max may not be the panacea for alternative governance for Scotland that many believe it could be.

Alternative status for the governance of Scotland: a return to Westminster

A survey conducted in 2017 by Panelbase for The Sunday Times found that many people were dissatisfied with the current status of the governance of devolution. The results found that less than half of voters believe devolution has improved Scotland's health and education service or its economy. 35% of those surveyed said that the provision and standard of healthcare has stayed the same since devolution, while 20% believe it has worsened. 26% believed that devolution has weakened the Scottish economy.

The survey of 1000 adults in Scotland also found that one in five voters — and one in three who voted against Scottish independence in 2014 — would rather abolish the Scottish parliament and return to being governed by London. This is significant as this shows that there is a growing movement of people in Scotland that would like to abolish devolution and return to full governance by Westminster. The 2017 Panelbase survey sampled only a tiny cohort of the Scottish population in 2017 (5,373,000) and so these results may not be entirely representative of the Scottish electorate to consider them to be significant.

Evaluation

It cannot be denied that the impact of the Brexit result will have far-reaching implications for Scotland. It is also the case that the campaigners for an independent Scotland may regard the result as unrepresentative of the wishes of the Scottish people and believe that the time for Indyref2 is imminent.

However, it may also be the case that there is little public appetite for another referendum and that some people have lost confidence in the political process in the post-Brexit era. Some people may feel that referenda results need to have a 'super majority' of 60% or more rather than a 'simple majority' of 50% or more.

The narrow defeat of the Scottish Independence Referendum in 2014 and the Brexit Referendum result highlight that massive political changes can come into effect with very narrow majorities. Indyref was rejected 55.3/44.7 with a turnout of 84.6%, NO won with only 46.8% of the registered Scottish electorate. Brexit was agreed by 51.9/48.1 with a turnout of 72.2%, Brexit was achieved by 37.47% of the registered British electorate.

The result has been a break down in societal cohesion, anger and frustration. It may be the case that this has led to political apathy among voters and as such calling Indyref2 soon would be an error of political judgement. Brexit has brought a great deal of uncertainty for the political, economic and social future of the UK as a whole and as such, clamours for devo-max, independence or even an abolishment of devolution and return to the governance of Scotland by Westminster, seem premature and undesirable at this point in time.

Implications of the UK's decision to leave the European Union (EU) or 'Brexit

Possible political implications

The political implications of Brexit on the UK and EU could be far-reaching.

The think tank, Institute for Government, reported in October 2018 that one significant area of political difficulties could be in relation to the relationship between the UK and Ireland. The UK and Ireland joined the European Economic Community at the same time in 1973, and their current economic and political relationship depends largely on their membership of the EU.

Areas of concern relate to the Good Friday Agreement signed in 1998 which brought an end to sectarian conflict and established power-sharing in Northern Ireland. This is significant as some critics of Brexit believe that leaving the EU will damage the sensitive political relationship between the UK and Northern Ireland.

Ian Blackford, the leader of the SNP at Westminster, claimed in January 2019 that the Conservative government had "reneged" on the UK's commitment to the Good Friday Agreement. The implication of this could be that the relationship between the UK and Northern Ireland could fragment further and potentially reignite the political violence of sectarian violence witnessed from the late 1960s, known as The Troubles. (The Troubles was a period of violence between two groups - Republicans (who wanted Northern Ireland to re-join the Republic) and Loyalists (who wanted to remain part of the UK). Many people were killed in the fighting.)

Another political implication could be that Brexit would weaken the UK's role on the global stage. Supporters of EU membership believe that Britain is stronger as part of the EU in terms of its ability to trade freely and benefit from certain laws.

It may also be the case that the UK's exit may reduce the influence of the EU as a whole. The EU will lose funding that was previously sourced from the UK resulting in other countries making up for this economic shortfall. The power balance within the EU may shift and some smaller member states are concerned that Brexit may embolden some stronger nations, such as Germany to dominate the organisation.

Possible economic implications

Researchers at the London School of Economics (LSE) claim that the range of economic consequences is broad.

It has been agreed broadly that there would be a short-term negative shock to the EU economy from Brexit. This is because of economic uncertainty and the resultant decrease in investment.

The Bank of England has warned that Brexit could result in financial instability that could have damaging economic effects because of the financial openness of the UK. The implication of this could be a decline in Gross Domestic Product (a measure of the value of the total production in a country. GDP is calculated by adding together total consumer spending, total government spending, total business spending, and the value of net exports) which could impact levels of employment, with job losses expected particularly in the car manufacturing and financial sectors. It could be argued, however that not all employment sectors could be affected by Brexit; it is possible that some sectors may see an increase in jobs.

In February 2019, a group of industry leaders known as the Institute of Directors (IOD) reported that 16% of UK businesses had already started the relocation process and another 13% were actively planning a move out of the UK. The loss of businesses from the UK could have a negative economic impact on the UK as this could result in a decline in GDP, unemployment and higher prices for consumers on goods being imported from other countries.

The Treasury warned that Brexit would lead to two quarters of negative growth that would last for a year and leave the level of UK GDP 3.6% lower in two years' time. The Treasury also predict that unemployment would be higher, wages 2.8% lower and house prices 10% down. This is significant as even though the UK may be saving on its current payments into the EU budget, any savings would be erased by the decline. It is possible that the UK may plunge into a shallow recession as a result of Brexit; the length of which is unknown.

Parts of the UK that benefit from EU regional policy would also lose the economic support they currently receive. West Wales & the Valleys and Cornwall & the Isles of Scilly are cases in point. The implication of this would be that unless the UK Government is able to replace this EU funding with domestic funding these regions will likely experience a decline in terms of business development, education and employment.

The Cornwall and Isles of Scilly Growth Programme was in line to receive £394million in development funds by 2020 – with £341 million allocated to Cornwall alone. A possible implication of a halt to this funding could be a decline in economic development and growth in regions such as this with undeveloped economies. Cornwall is set to lose £60 million of annual funding from the EU and claims that it was promised replacement funding from the UK Government. Interestingly almost 60% of voters in Cornwall voted to leave the EU despite the economic benefits the region enjoyed as a result of EU funding. The Department for Communities and Local

Government has given Cornwall and the Isles of Scilly Local Enterprise Partnership (LEP) just a fraction of the £127 million it had originally sought.

RAND Europe report that the option of leaving the EU with no deal and simply applying World Trade Organization (WTO) rules would lead to the greatest economic losses for the UK. The analysis of this particular scenario shows that trading under WTO rules would reduce future GDP by around 5% ten years after Brexit, or $140 billion, compared with EU membership.

Potential social implications

There will be significant implications for patient healthcare and public health as a result of the UK's decision to leave the EU.

The National Health Service (NHS) has long been reliant on EU workers, with around 10% of doctors and 5% of nurses originated from other EU member states. It has been estimated that if health and social care workers are considered together, there are around 200,000 EU nationals working in the sector. The uncertainty posed by the Brexit negotiations to date has already affected staffing levels.

The Royal College of Nursing reported a 92% drop in registrations of nurses from the EU member states in England in March 2017 and attributed this to "the failure of the government to provide EU nationals in the UK with any security about their future". The possible implications of the UK's decision to leave the EU could be that the NHS will struggle to fill vacancies of departing EU nationals working in the sector if they are forced or decide to leave.

Unless the UK Government makes significant strides to increase the numbers of UK-trained health and social care workers there will be an impact on the quality and ability of the NHS to deliver on its core principles of meeting the needs of everyone and providing free health care at the point of delivery.

The UK is currently part of the European Medicines Agency, which regulates the approval of medicines to be placed on the EU market. It is unclear whether the UK will be able to participate in this system on leaving the EU. The implication of this could be that the NHS could experience a shortage of medical supplies and an increase in costs to the NHS.

It could also mean that some innovative treatments may not be available on the UK market which could have serious implications for patient care and mortality rates.

One other area that will be impacted by Brexit is collaborative clinical research. UK organisations are the largest beneficiary of EU health research funds in Europe, with €760 million in EU funding having supported research in the UK between 2007 and 2013. There has been a reluctance to include the UK in EU-funded health projects as a result of the UK's decision to leave the EU.

The implications of this is that the UK will not be able to innovate at the same rate as other EU organisations and perhaps, as a result, will not attract the best clinicians due to a lack of opportunity and funding. This will have a direct impact on patient care and wellbeing as research may not develop at the rate at which it would in a collaborative setting. Professor Jonathan Adams, writing in 2017 for 'UK in a Changing Europe' (a non-partisan website funded by the Economic and Social Research Council (ESRC), and based at King's College London), claimed that "with less European collaboration after Brexit, access to shared ideas and endeavour will be more limited, access to added capacity and specialist facilities will be restricted, and the average impact of UK research will fall."

Elisabetta Zanon, director of the NHS European Office warned that there may be significant implications for public health as a result of Brexit.

Zanon points to the fact that the EU has an early warning and response system for potential public health threats, such as the Zika virus, coordinated by the European Centre for Disease Prevention and Control. This system allows EU/EEA member states to easily share information, pool resources for lab investigations and work together to develop new strategies for future threats. There is a possibility that on leaving the EU, the UK will be excluded from this coordination system. The consequences of this would be delays in communication, action and serious public health implications.

Under current EU law, EU citizens benefit from rights to reciprocal healthcare when they are in any of the European Union's 28 member states. The Brexit Health Alliance is campaigning for continued access to reciprocal healthcare rights post-Dec 2020. The future of healthcare for UK citizens travelling and holidaying in EU countries remains uncertain.

Evaluation

Overall, the implications of the UK's decision to leave the EU is largely unknown at this stage. It could be argued that on one hand there will be a short-term economic downturn, but there is a real likelihood that the economy will recover again. Brexiteers have put forward the argument that the UK has the capacity to build a competitive economy outside the EU and that since the UK retained its own currency rather than join the Eurozone, its economy is not going to struggle to adjust in the long-term. It could also be the case that some industries will return to the UK to reinvigorate the economies of once-prosperous parts of the country. Fishing and agriculture may benefit from not being constrained in some respects by the Common Agricultural and Fishing Policies. It is also possible that trade deals with other countries and continents such as Africa may be easier to win as a result of the UK's decision to leave the EU. Some commentators believe that without EU interference the UK would be able to nationalise key industries such as steel, which could result in the safeguarding of employment in this essential industry. In addition, some argue that the UK's national sovereignty will be restored as a result of Brexit. The UK will no longer be beholden to the EU's directives, taxes and laws. Sovereignty allows a state to wield absolute power to govern itself, make, execute, and apply laws, and impose and collect taxes. It will be the case that as the UK leaves the European Union, the sovereignty of the UK Government will be restored.

It could also be argued that the UK's decision to leave the EU will result in a domino effect of other member states seeking to leave or re-negotiate their terms of membership. It could also be the case that this may result in the break-up of the EU as an international organisation and this would have a negative impact on the Euro currency.

What is certain is that the UK must seek to ensure that issues surrounding medical care and research are analysed and tackled carefully. It may be the case that the UK Government could attract investment for research and clinical trials from other countries, such as the USA or China. With new sources of funding the UK may be able to ensure the safety of public health and safeguard against shortages of medical supplies.

veness of parliamentary
ives in holding the government to
unt.

An important part of a democracy is the ability of parliamentary representatives (Members of Parliament and Members of the House of Lords) to hold the government, or executive, to account for their actions or inactions. The main ways that the government can be held to account are:

- Asking questions of Prime Minister, Theresa May during the weekly televised Prime Minister's Question Time.
- The role of the opposition (Currently this is the Labour Party) in forming a shadow cabinet to monitor the actions and policies of the government.
- Select Committees that scrutinise or check the policies and decision making of the government.

Prime Minister's Questions

Each Wednesday at noon, MPs are able to pose questions to the Prime Minister. This is known as Prime Minister's Questions or PMQs and lasts for half an hour. There are two purposes for parliamentary questions: to seek information from ministers and to press them for action.

The leader of the opposition, currently Sir Keir Starmer, Leader of the Labour Party, has the right to ask six questions of the Prime Minister, Boris Johnson. Starmer is the only parliamentary representative that is permitted to respond to Johnson with further questions. The leader of the third-largest party in the Commons is permitted to ask two questions. These questions do not have to be shown to the Prime Minister in advance.

A ballot is held for other MPs and if they are selected by random, they may pose their question. Unlike questions tabled to other ministers, there is no requirement to provide advance notice of the question to be asked. This is important as is shows that the government can be held to account by parliamentary representatives in a public forum. While the Prime Minister may not know all of the questions in advance, she will be extensively briefed by government departments in anticipation of likely subjects that she could be asked about. Some questions posed may cause the Prime Minister embarrassment, some questions will not be answered satisfactorily while others will be posed by the governing party in order to flatter the Prime Minister. While PMQs is a way for parliamentary representatives to scrutinise the government, it could be argued that it is limited in its effectiveness as questions can be rebuffed, not all are answered fully and some questions and answers are merely about scoring political points rather than scrutinising the actions of the government.

In September 2016, Jeremy Corbyn asked the Prime Minister at PMQs whether any experts backed her policy on grammar schools:

"I wonder if it is possible for her this morning, within the quiet confines of this House, to name any educational experts who back her proposals on new grammar schools and more selection," he asked.

The Prime Minister responded:

"I am glad that the right hon. Gentleman has raised the issue of education, because it enables me to point out that over the past six years, we have seen 1.4 million more children in good or outstanding schools. That is because of the changes that this Government introduced: free schools and academies, head teachers being put in charge of schools, and more choice for parents. I note that the right hon. Gentleman has opposed all those changes. What I want to see is more good school places and a diversity of provision of education in this country so that we really see opportunity for all and young people going as far as their talents will take them."

This shows clearly that while the leader of the opposition has the opportunity to hold the Prime Minister and her government to account about policy matters, questions can be avoided and answers can be twisted to fit the political agenda that the Prime Minister wishes to advance.

The role of the opposition

The leader of the largest opposition party is the Leader of the Official Opposition. This is currently the Labour Party.

Rt Hon Jeremy Corbyn MP, was the Leader of the Official Opposition from 2015-2020. Sir Keir Starmer became the Leader of the Official Opposition in April 2020 when he won the leadership of the Labour Party. The Leader of the Official Opposition picks a 'Shadow Cabinet' to follow the work of government departments. The current Home Secretary is Priti Patel (Conservative). The current shadow Home Secretary is Nick Thomas-Symonds (Labour).   In this role, Ms Patel is responsible for matters relating to security and terrorism, the legislative programme and expenditure issues.

In July 2020, the two MPs clashed over the UK Government's plans to introduce a points-based immigration system. Under the government's plans when the Brexit transition period ends, those wishing to live and work in the UK must gain 70 points. There is a mandatory requirement for visa applicants to have an offer of a job on a list of eligible occupations and speak English - earning them 50 points. There is a minimum salary requirement of £20,480.

Further points would be awarded for meeting criteria such as holding a PhD relevant to the job or earning more than a "general salary threshold" of £25,600. The health and care visa will be open to workers who have a confirmed job offer in one of a series of "skilled" roles within the NHS or care sector - or for NHS service providers, such as doctors, nurses, radiographers, social workers and paramedics. Unions have criticised the exclusion of frontline care home workers and contractors and pointing out that a minimum salary threshold means that many cleaners, porters and support staff would also not qualify.

Shadow home secretary Nick Thomas-Symonds said: "To exclude care workers from the health visa is a clear signal that this government does not appreciate the skill and dedication these roles involve... it is yet another insult from this Tory party to those who have been at the frontline of this crisis."

Labour said it would scrutinise the proposals "very carefully", saying the government had "rushed through immigration legislation with very little detail in the middle of a global pandemic".

This shows that the shadow cabinet can be an effective way in which the work of the government can be scrutinised as each shadow minister can examine closely the work of each government department and develop policies in their specific areas. Shadow ministers are ideally placed to follow carefully the work of their counterpart in the Cabinet and can therefore hold to account the government for their policies and actions. Shadow ministers will use the media to highlight concerns and this can also facilitate government scrutiny.

Given that the current Conservative government boasts the majority of MPs in the House of Commons, it has the ability to set the political agenda and pass legislation it wishes either through a vote in the Commons or through secondary legislation known as statutory instruments (SIs) where an existing law is amended or information is added by ministers (or other bodies) under powers given to them by an Act of Parliament.

This removes the requirement for the reading of a Bill. This means that it can be difficult for the opposition to scrutinise legislation being passed. There are approximately 3,500 SIs made each year, although only about 1,000 need to be considered by Parliament. Parliament can either approve or reject an SI but cannot amend it. 80% of SIs are laid out under what is known as the negative procedure. Negative SIs do not need active approval by Parliament. Usually negative SIs are signed by the minister before being laid in Parliament.

An SI laid under the negative procedure becomes law on the day the Minister signs it and automatically remains law unless a motion – or 'prayer' – to reject it is agreed by either House within 40 sitting days. This shows clearly that SIs laid out under the negative procedure are difficult to reject and in fact a successful motion to stop SIs is rare.

This means that the ability of the opposition to scrutinise the government can be hindered and ineffective when holding the government to account over secondary legislation. It could also be argued that these powers of the government are undemocratic as it removes the need for parliamentary approval, and it damages the concept of parliamentary sovereignty.

In February 2019 eight Labour MPs resigned from the Party. The seven Labour defectors - Chuka Umunna, Luciana Berger, Chris Leslie, Angela Smith, Mike Gapes, Gavin Shuker, Ann Coffey and Joan Ryan - quit the party in protest at what they said was a culture of "bullying and bigotry" in the party, a culture of anti-Semitism and frustration over the leadership's reluctance to back another EU referendum. This is significant as it could be argued that the opposition is ineffective at scrutinising the government because of its internal conflicts which have detracted from its role of holding the government to account.

The role of Select Committees

Select committees are responsible for scrutinising the work of government. They have the capacity to hold to account the decision-making of the government and call upon individuals to answer criticisms. Select Committees work in both the House of Commons and the House of Lords. They will conduct investigations, write reports and provide recommendations.

The results of these inquiries are public, and many require a response from the government. One example of the work of a Select Committee is the Foreign Affairs Committee Enquiry (2016) which investigated the UK's actions in Libya in 2011. As part of the protest movement in the Middle East, beginning in Tunisia in December 2010, demonstrations commenced in Libya on 15 February 2011, when anti-Gaddafi protests erupted in Benghazi. By the end of February 2011, the Gaddafi regime had lost control of a significant part of Libya, including the major cities of Misrata and Benghazi. 5.

In March 2011, pro-Gaddafi forces launched a counter-offensive against the rebels that reached the outskirts of Benghazi. In response, the United Nations Security Council agreed Resolution 1973 on 17 March, which authorised member states to establish and enforce a no-fly zone over Libya and to use "all necessary measures" to prevent attacks on civilians. A coalition of nations including the UK and USA contributed military assets to enforce Resolution 1973. Parliament approved the UK's participation in the military intervention following a debate on 21 March 2011 by a vote of 557 to 13.

The Foreign Affairs Committee appointed Professor Toby Dodge, London School of Economics, as a Specialist Adviser at the start of the 2015 Parliament to provide ongoing advice on events in the Middle East. In addition, it engaged Joseph Walker-Cousins, the former Head of the British Embassy Office in Benghazi, to act as Specialist Adviser for this particular inquiry.

The Committee heard from all but one of the key British protagonists involved in the decision to intervene in Libya in 2011. It invited the then Prime Minister right hon. David Cameron MP to provide oral evidence to the inquiry in March 2016. He declined this invitation citing "the pressures on his diary". The Committee members visited North Africa in March 2016, when they met Libyan politicians along with Egyptian and Tunisian politicians and policymakers. The Committee concluded:

"We have seen no evidence that the UK Government carried out a proper analysis of the nature of the rebellion in Libya. It may be that the UK Government was unable to analyse the nature of the rebellion in Libya due to incomplete intelligence and insufficient institutional insight and that it was caught up in events as they developed. It could not verify the actual threat to civilians posed by the Gaddafi regime; it selectively took elements of Muammar Gaddafi's rhetoric at face value; and it failed to identify the militant Islamist extremist element in the rebellion. UK strategy was founded on erroneous assumptions and an incomplete understanding of the evidence."

The House of Commons Liaison Committee is made up of Select Committee Chairs. It considers the overall work of select committees, promotes effective scrutiny of Government, and chooses committee reports for debates. It questions the Prime Minister about policy, usually three times a year. In May 2020 the Committee questioned Johnson about the government's handling of the Covid-19 pandemic and the actions of his senior adviser, Dominic Cummings and his alleged breaking of the lockdown rules.

Select Committees are often regarded as one of the most effective strategies that parliamentary representatives can hold the government to account. This is because they investigate government policies and legislation among other important issues. They have the ability to hold government ministers to account and urge them to respond to their recommendations.

The Government will normally make a response within two months of the publication of the Committee's report. This can be considered an effective form of scrutiny as many of these committees are high profile and attract a great deal of media attention. This can often push government ministers to respond and act according to the recommendations that the Committee has made.

Writing for the London School of Economics and Political Science (LSE), The Hansard Society's Matt Korris claims that, "Select committees are one of the great success stories of Parliament. Over the last 30 years they have become the principal mechanism through which the House of Commons holds the executive to account and have influenced the direction of government policy and legislation". However, Korris also claims that the Committees face an increasing workload which can make effective scrutiny difficult.

He also claims that committees should focus on how they follow-up their work and recommendations: "The current model encourages committees to undertake inquiries, hold hearings and produce reports, but then often leave the subject entirely and move on to other things. Committees should seek to maintain a watching brief on areas they have scrutinised, examining whether their recommendations have been implemented, and calling ministers to fresh evidence sessions to account for progress." This indicates that although the Select Committees do perform an important role in holding the government to account it can be the case that their recommendations are not followed up and since they do not have any legal powers to ensure that individuals appear before them, their ability to scrutinise effectively is limited.

Evaluation

It would be fair to suggest that there are ways in which the government can be held to account or scrutinised by parliamentary representatives. While PMQs can offer a public means through which MPs can question the Prime Minister, it could be argued that this is more parliamentary theatre and about political point scoring than true and effective scrutiny. Furthermore, the role of the opposition should be to act as a viable government-in-waiting monitoring government actions in terms of policy, legislation and expenditure among other issues.

Without a strong opposition party, it could be argued that effective scrutiny is not possible and the current Labour party's ability to scrutinise the government has been overshadowed by its own issues surrounding anti-Semitism and bullying. An opposition party riven with in-fighting and breaking apart is not an effective body through which effective scrutiny can be achieved. Therefore, of all the vehicles through which scrutiny can be achieved, the Select committees should be considered the most effective, even with their clear limitations.

If the committees are able to follow-up more rigorously on their own recommendations it is possible that real and effective scrutiny of the government could take place.

It is certainly the case that when high-profile investigations of the Select Committees are publicised in the media and therefore become public knowledge, scrutiny of the government can take place and ministers can be forced to act upon the recommendations made by the committees.

The strengths and weaknesses of different electoral systems used in elections within the UK.

The main electoral systems used within the UK are First Past the Post for general elections to the Westminster Parliament, Additional Member System, used to elect MSPs to the Scottish Parliament and Single Transferable Vote, used to elect councillors in Scottish local government elections.

It is important to evaluate each electoral system in terms of its fairness, complexity and ability to represent the people in order to ascertain their strengths and weaknesses.

First Past the Post

The UK's main electoral system, first past the post (FPTP), is a traditional electoral system that sees the UK divided into 650 constituencies of similar size populations. Voters vote for the candidate they want; this candidate represents a political party or may be independent of a political party. The candidate that gains the most votes is elected MP for that constituency seat. Under FPTP, the party that wins the most seats forms the government.

One benefit of FPTP is that voters can clearly express their view on which party they think should form the next government. The fact that the majority of those registered to vote have the opportunity to vote means that everyone has the chance to have their political view represented by an MP in parliament, showing how FPTP can in fact be representative.

Another way in which it could be argued that FPTP is representative, is that it promotes clarity, making it extremely easy for voters to understand the system. This would perhaps improve representation as it could mean that people are more likely to vote if they understand the system.

As a result, voter turnout could increase, and the election result could be deemed to be more representative of the will of the people. However, in practice, FPTP often results in many people being under-represented. One example is how in the 2015 general election the Conservative Party won 36.9% of the vote share and were able to form a majority government.

This shows how FPTP is unrepresentative as it resulted in 2/3 of the UK electorate being under-represented. Furthermore, FPTP leads to one representative being elected to represent one constituency, for example, John Nicolson (SNP) was elected MP (Conservative) for Ochil and South Perthshire in December 2019.

The MP can represent his or her constituents by posing questions in the House of Commons, sitting on committees and taking part in debates. This means that there is a direct link between the MP and the constituents which could lead to people feeling represented in the Westminster Parliament as the MP works on issues relating to employment, for example, in the constituency.

In the 2017 General Election, Luke Graham MP gained around 22,000 votes while the candidate that came in second place, Tasmina Ahmed-Sheikh (SNP) gained around 19,000.

Since FPTP is a 'winner takes all' electoral system, the 19,000 people that voted for Ms Ahmed Sheikh will feel underrepresented by Mr Graham. Almost 11,000 votes were cast for the Labour candidate and 1,700 votes were cast for the Liberal Democrats in this constituency.

This means that more people did not vote for the elected MP, Luke Graham, than did vote for him. Because he gained around 6% more votes than the second-place candidate, he was elected as the MP.

MPs can win by tiny margins as was seen again in 2017 when the SNP's Stephen Gethins became the MP for North East Fife, winning by just two votes. This shows that while FPTP offers a clear electoral system that is simple to understand, it can lead to underrepresentation of the electorate as the majority of votes could be regarded as wasted.

In the 2019 General Election, some of the seats proved to be a very close call. Fermanagh and South Tyrone saw the smallest majority as Sinn Féin's Michelle Gildernew held onto her seat with a 57 vote majority over Ulster Unionist Party.

Furthermore, according to the 2011 report by the Institute of Public Policy Research, not only does FPTP fail the "fairness test" by generating major discrepancies between the number of votes secured and the proportion of seats won in the House of Commons but, as the outcome of the 2010 general election proves FPTP can no longer claim to guarantee "strong single party government." This is because it resulted in a coalition between the Conservatives and Lib Dems which was largely unsuccessful.

This shows that people may be under-represented using this electoral system because not only is the relationship between the number of votes and number of seats disproportionate but if a coalition government is formed people's political views are not being represented as coalition governments often have antagonistic views and can struggle pass legislation.

This stagnation can result in a lack of representation of the people and this is undemocratic as elected representatives are in office to represent the people. Another example of how FPTP is unrepresentative is that in the 2015 general election UKIP received 3.8 million votes, which under the current voting system equated to one seat. This is because UKIP came second in around 120 constituencies and with a winner takes all electoral system such as FPTP, these votes, were in effect, wasted. Almost 4 million people therefore were significantly under-represented.

This shows that FPTP is unrepresentative as one in every 7 people in England voted for UKIP and the party received 12.7% of the vote share, yet these people were not represented adequately in parliament which shows how unfair and unrepresentative this system can be.

Under FPTP, parties are also being under-represented in Westminster. An example of this can be seen in how it took 25,283 votes to elect a single SNP MP in 2015 to Westminster whereas it took 3.5 million votes to elect a single UKIP MP in 2015. This is because the SNP wields strong regional support in Scotland and Scottish MPs have 59 seats ring-fenced or reserved for them in Westminster.

This means that parties that do not have strong regional support will struggle to gain representation and this therefore shows how unrepresentative and unfair FPTP is as an electoral system.

FPTP also creates 'safe seats' where the result is an inevitable win for one of the parties. Nearly 14 million voters are in seats that have not changed party hands since the Second World War, according to research by the Electoral Reform Society.

This shows that FPTP is not very fair or representative because people feel trapped with the same representation for decades and this is not the hallmark of a responsive and full democracy.

Additional Member System

Additional Member System is a hybrid electoral system used in the Welsh Assembly and Scottish Parliament. It is thought to be much more representative of the electorate than First Past the Post because it allows voters two votes through which they can express a preference for both a candidate and a party rather than just a candidate as is the case in a FPTP voting system.

Under AMS each party receives roughly the same percentage of available seats in Parliament as the percentage of votes cast for the party. This is in direct contrast to First Past the Post in that the party with the most votes becomes the majority government and there are many votes wasted. As a result of this many voters feel underrepresented. Under AMS, however, voters may feel more represented because they are able to vote for a single constituency representative and a party of their choice. AMS is used successfully in the Scottish Parliament where there are 129 seats available for MSPs.

In the 2016 Scottish General Election, the SNP received 47% of the constituency vote share and took 59 seats. It won 42% of the regional vote and gained 4 regional seats bring the party's total seats in Parliament to 63. This shows that the number of seats won is roughly proportional to the party's vote share and therefore more representative. Labour won 23% of the constituency vote share and took 3 seats and 19% of the regional vote gaining 21 seats.

Using the D'hondt method of counting votes where the number of votes cast is divided by the number of constituency and regional seats +1 we can argue this result is roughly proportional but certainly far more proportional than FPTP.

Therefore, AMS can be considered far more representative of the electorate than FPTP. This is clearly more representative as political representatives and political parties receive a more proportional amount of seats in relation to the amount of votes that they won.

AMS is more representative than a winner takes all system such as FPTP because it allows greater political diversity and more minority parties have a greater chance of being represented. AMS can be regarded as more representative than FPTP as there is more scope for a broader range of voices, issues, ethnicities and genders to be heard and seen in Parliament.

This is significant because this is much more representative of the people and as a result fewer political voices or parties are marginalised. In fact, even independent candidates have a greater chance of being successful under AMS as they can be added as either a constituency MSP or an "additional member". This is important as this enhances the democratic process and ensures that there will not be a dominance of only two main political parties.

Overall, AMS can prevent a minority rule government as is seen under FPTP and the 2015 General Election Result for the UK Parliament when the Conservatives became the government with only 37% of the vote share.

It could be argued that AMS as a system of Proportional Representation would have dramatically altered the result of the 2015 UK General Election. The reason for this is that although the Conservatives would have remained the biggest party, parties such as UKIP would have won 82 seats rather than the 1 seat it held in 2015 in Parliament.

The Green Party would also have increased their number of seats to 24. This shows that AMS as a form of Proportional Representation is far more representative of the people and their voting decisions however as an electoral system, AMS is more complicated than FPTP and this could result in a higher proportion of spoilt ballot papers as people may vote in error. This could result in lower participation in the political process and this could then bring to power an unrepresentative government.

Finally, it could be argued that a system of AMS could result in a coalition government which be considered to be more representative of the people. The reason for this is that coalitions can encourage democratic debate and avoid governments elected on small percentages such as the Conservative Government in 2015.

However, an argument against this is that coalitions can result in slow progress as several parties may struggle to agree on matters and this can then hinder progress. This can mean that no party can pass legislation and so the people are not represented.

Single Transferable Vote

Single Transferable Vote (STV) presents the electorate with a greater chance of representation than any other electoral system, particularly hybrid systems such as AMS or a "winner takes all" system such as FPTP. This system puts most power in the hands of the voters.

Voters can rank candidates by number according to their preference. There is a far greater choice of political parties, representatives and independent candidates in an STV electoral system. This could ensure that a diversity of opinion, gender, ethnicity is reflected, making this system far more representative than FPTP or AMS.

There are no wasted votes in an STV system as if a voter's favourite candidate (ranked '1') has enough votes to win a seat already and has reached the required quota of votes, the vote is transferred to the voter's second, or third choice candidate.

This is significant as it shows STV is a representative system as voters of not have to be concerned about whether their party will win enough votes, they can express their true political view which will be represented by MPS and parties. This allows more candidates to be put forward and also prevents the marginalisation of females and ethnic minorities who are often under-represented in parliament under FPTP, showing how this would be a more representative electoral system that FPTP.

Furthermore, there is no need for tactical voting in the Single Transferable Voting electoral system. STV is representative as people do not have to worry about who everyone else is voting for, and if it will affect their party of choice, voters just have to vote for the party they favour, which is of critical importance as if people do not vote tactically their political views will be reflected in parliament. This will result in a more representative government.

The 2017 local government Scottish elections results showed that under STV, smaller parties are more likely to be represented. For example, currently the Green Party has 5 councillors across Glasgow City Council and 14 in Scotland as a whole. Under an FPTP system the Greens would have had little chance of gaining representatives at council level. Independent councillors retained majority control over the 3 island councils in 2017. This shows that STV increases the opportunity for more marginal parties and independent voices to be heard in local politics which means that STV could be regarded as fairer and more representative of the electorate.

In 2012, the SNP gained 32% of first choice votes and were awarded 35% of councillors across Scotland. Labour had 32% of first choice votes and gained 32% of councillors across Scotland. This shows how STV is representative as it shows a broadly proportional result, emphasising the effectiveness of this system in representing the voters.

Overall it is clear that STV is the most representative of all three systems, as it gives people a choice from a multitude of representatives, unlike FPTP, and means there is no wasted votes, unlike STV, proving that is it is the most representative electoral system.

There are no safe seats in STV so this will encourage more people to actually engage with politics because the result is not already inevitable. This is significant as it shows that STV could be more representative of the people especially when compared to FPTP. The Electoral Reform Society points to the issue of safe seats and estimated that there are hundreds of seats that have been held continually by one political party since the 19th century.

Safe seats for the Conservative Party tend to be in rural areas and the Home Counties. In the absence of safe seats in an STV electoral system, political parties must work harder for their votes, and campaign everywhere, not just in marginal seats as there are no safe seats, meaning people will have a clearer indication of who it is they support, which will give rise to a more democratic and fair electoral system which has been proven to work extremely well in Scottish local government elections.

Evaluation

Overall, it would be fair to evaluate that STV is by far the most fair and representative especially when compared to the alterative electoral systems of AMS and FPTP. It could be argued that since there are no wasted votes or safe seats and a greater chance of marginalised voices gaining representation in local government elections, STV is the most superior electoral system.

That said, this system's complexity may decrease voter turnout or increase the number of spoiled ballot papers, which would ultimately reduce the chances of gaining a representative council.

However, all things considered if STV were adopted as the electoral system for the general elections to the Westminster Parliament, it would radically shake up national politics. It would increase the likelihood of coalition governments which while being more representative, could struggle to pass legislation due to the number of competing views and agendas.

However, MPs would not be able to be elected on tiny majorities and voters may feel much more represented as a result. AMS is more representative than FPTP but since the first vote is undertaken using FPTP, it cannot be considered to be the fairest electoral system.

FPTP, although simple to grasp as an electoral system is not representative and can result in governments forming with very small majorities, leaving the majority of the electorate un-represented.

Factors which influence voting behaviour including class, age and media.

Age

According to the independent research organisation, Democratic Audit, there is a gradual gravitation as people age towards parties that defend the status quo and claim to offer socio-economic stability. This means that it is likely to be the Conservative Party that benefits from Britain's 'ageing society' as older people who are keen to maintain stability in their lives are attracted to their message of 'Strong and Stable Government'.

Given that older people are more likely to turn out to vote and are more likely to vote for the Conservatives, it is unsurprising that this party won the 2015 General Election, and the subsequent 2017 General Election.

When David Cameron formed his Conservative government in 2015, he promised to maintain the 'triple lock' on state pensions which means that they will rise in line with prices, earnings or 2.5 %, whichever is highest. He also affirmed a commitment to keep a raft of universal benefits that pensioners receive such as winter fuel allowances and free bus passes.

This is significant as this shows that the Conservative Party understand their core voter and are careful to create manifesto pledges that attract them. It could be argued that as people age, they become more risk averse and therefore their voting behaviour could be heavily influenced by a desire and a political party that is defined by an ideology of 'rootedness', paternalism and pragmatism.

There was a clear generational divide on Brexit in relation to the age of voters and the rate at which they turned out in the EU Referendum held in June 2016. The result of the referendum was found to be in favour of the UK leaving the EU with 48.1% voting for the UK to remain in the EU and 51.9% voting to leave.

Of these voters, 61% of males aged 18-24 and 80% of females of the same age group voted to remain in the EU. Just over 60% of males aged 60+ voted to leave the EU and this was broadly the same for females of the same age, although 66% of females 65+ voted to leave the EU.

This is significant as it shows that in the case of the Brexit Referendum, age was clearly a determining factor in voting behaviour. While age demographic groups cannot be considered homogenous, it would still be fair to analyse this data as evidence of age influencing voting behaviour. That said, it could also be the case that the voting behaviour seen in the EU Referendum was influenced by other more significant factors, such as identity politics, fears about immigration and misinformation about the vast sums of money that could be spent on the NHS if the UK was to be liberated from its EU membership. People in relatively prosperous regions such as London supported 'remain', whereas people in poorer areas such as the North-East of England opted to leave, and therefore, geographic location, not simply age may have had a significant and simultaneous impact on voting behaviour in this referendum.

YouGov analysis of voting behaviour in 2017 found that "age seems to be the new dividing line in British politics".

The international Internet-based market research and data analytics firm found that amongst first time voters (those aged 18 and 19), Labour was forty-seven percentage points ahead. Amongst those aged over 70, the Conservatives had a lead of fifty percentage points. This shows that younger people were attracted to the policies of Jeremy Corbyn's Labour Party. Corbyn committed to invest in the NHS, social care, housing and education, funded in part by taxing the wealthy. Labour's commitment to make university tuition fees also helped to attract a younger demographic as this latter policy was particularly relevant to the first- time voters in 2017.

Many younger voters were attracted by Corbyn's call for social action and greater equality and less attracted by the Tory commitment to slash the welfare spending budget by ending the government provision of universal free school meals (free school meals are now means-tested).

It may also be the case that the voting behaviour of younger voters is not yet driven or influenced strongly by concerns about income tax, inflation rates, inheritance tax and pensions. As a result, younger voters are more likely to vote for a political party that represents their lives and lifestyles and less likely to vote for a party that they feel may not represent their immediate needs and aspirations.

57% of 18 and 19-year-olds voted in the 2017 General Election, for those aged 70+ the figure was 84%. Therefore, it must be concluded that age may have a significant influence on voting behaviour with younger voters less likely to turn out to vote and older voters more likely to turn out to vote.

This might be because younger people can be less settled in their lifestyles while older voters may be more stable and be more impacted by general election results. It could also be the case that older voters regard voting as a social norm and civic duty and may value the right to vote more highly that younger people.

While this is a significant generalisation of behaviour, it may be true that some older people remember times when their relatives did not enjoy the franchise and had to fight for the right to vote. This may explain the higher turnout rates for older people as they may appreciate its importance in a different way to younger people who have never known a time in which voting was not universal for those over 18.

Media

New Media

Political parties nationally spent about £1.3m on Facebook advertising during the 2015 general election campaign; two years later the figure soared to £3.2m. It has been found that in the run up to the 2015 and 2017 general elections it was the Conservative Party that spent the most.

In the run up to the 2015 General election, the Conservatives spent £1.2 million on Facebook advertising; Labour spent a fraction of this figure directly on Facebook. The Conservatives also spent £312,033 on Google advertising, compared to Labour's £371. The Conservative Party employed experienced digital strategists and as a result developed a range of video adverts on YouTube.

Given that the Conservative Party won both the 2015 and 2017 general elections it could be argued that new media has played a significant role in influencing voting behaviour.

This is because as print newspaper readership declines, and social media use increases, the electorate could feasibly determine their political compass while scrolling social media platforms. Due to the ability of advertisers to target directly certain demographic groups using Facebook advertising at a relatively low cost, political parties find that social media adverts and videos can be directed at voters, particularly in marginal constituencies. Such 'bitesize' chunks of simple text and image or video offers the voter an immediate understanding of the message being delivered.

In 2018 the Office of National Statistics (ONS) reported that 90% of adults in the UK were recent internet users, up from 89% in 2017, 8.4% of adults had never used the internet in 2018, down from 9.2% in 2017 and virtually all adults aged 16 to 34 years were recent internet users (99%), compared with 44% of adults aged 75 years and over. Twitter is used by all political parties to influence voting behaviour.

As of January 2019, Nicola Sturgeon, leader of the SNP and First Minister enjoyed a Twitter following of almost 1 million; Jeremy Corbyn had almost 2 million Twitter followers and Teresa May (Twitter handle: @10DowningStreet) had 5.5 million followers. It is via these 280-character messages that political parties and figures can reach out to the electorate very quickly and possibly influence their voting behaviour. People can contact these individuals publicly and often scrutinise their actions or inaction. This can help to inform voting behaviour.

Online political campaigning in the run up to elections or referenda can be beneficial to parties as there is no ban on political advertising online as there is on television. Jeremy Corbyn praised social media as an alternative way to reach big audiences. He wrote on his Facebook page in May 2016: "When in one week, we can get 1m-2m people watching online a message . . . it is a way of reaching past the censorship of the right-wing media in this country that has so constrained political debate for so long." This shows that social media has the capacity to be hugely influential on voting behaviour as its reach is broad and political messages could 'go viral' which could help provide momentum and interest in a political party.

Labour made effective use of hashtags on their social media platforms to generate momentum and galvanise the youth into political action through memes and other images. For example, #VoteLabour (83,094 posts) and #ForTheManyNotTheFew (20,063 posts). Researchers at Oxford University found that young voters were not only more visible on social media in 2017, but they were also more left-leaning and more likely to put their faith in political parties that support globalisation. This is significant as it shows that social media may have had a notable impact on voting behaviour, particularly among younger voters as turnout among this demographic rose significantly during 2017 General Election and it was reported that 63% of 18–34-year olds voted Labour.

Ed Balls, the former UK shadow chancellor said that a well-organised social media "surge" can recruit members and generate excitement faster than ever before. "But social media cannot begin to explain, at root, why politics today is in such turmoil. It is a magnifier of events, but it doesn't change the fundamentals."

Charlie Beckett, professor of media and politics at London School of Economics, says platforms such as Twitter are political bubbles rather than megaphones. "Twitter can't be used to identify swing voters and nudge them to vote for you."

It could certainly be the case that social media's influence on voting behaviour is relatively limited as platforms such as Twitter, which tend to be dominated by a left-wing voice, can act as an echo chamber rather than a creator or influencer of political viewpoints.

Newspapers

Newspapers in the UK do not have any restrictions on editorial bias towards political parties and are traditionally partisan in their approach to politics. YouGov conducted a survey of just over 50,000 adults in the UK about the newspapers they read and how they voted in 2017.

The results revealed that of those surveyed, 79% of Telegraph readers voted for the Conservatives and 73% of Guardian readers voted for Labour. This would suggest that print media may have an influence on voting behaviour as these figures reveal a clear correlation between partisan print media and party affiliation.

That said, print media readership is experiencing a decline and considering that younger voters do not tend to get their news and opinions from newspapers, it would be fair to suggest that the influence of newspapers on voting behaviour is limited. It may be the case that people that read newspapers will select publications and headlines that reflect their pre-existing political standpoints and opinions.

What is interesting to note is that of the people surveyed by YouGov, 12% of Telegraph readers voted Labour. This seems at odds with the political affiliation of the Telegraph which is also known as the 'Torygraph'.

This would indicate that people are perhaps not influenced by the print media but are more influenced by single issues such as Brexit, environmental issues or a desire to keep out another political party with a strategic vote.

Television

TV was the most effective media in influencing people's votes in the build up to the 2015 General Election, with 62% of the electorate claiming it had been influential, while social media was only deemed persuasive by 11% of voters, according to research from Otherlines.tv.

Of those voters who said TV was influential, 61% were swayed by live political debates, 38% by national news, but a mere 16% by party political broadcasts. This is significant as this research shows the significant impact that television can have in influencing voting behaviour.

The ITV leaders' debates in particular were very influential perhaps became the leaders could demonstrate their authenticity and even humour. The TV debates feel like a live competition and an exposure of personalities. Perhaps in this era of endless talent shows on TV, the debates felt akin to these oftentimes ruthless contests which are so popular with the general population.

Class

It was the case in pre-1980s Britain that people tended to vote along class lines. This is known as 'class alignment'. ABC1s would vote for the Conservative Party and C2DE tended to vote Labour.

There is evidence (post-1980s) of class-dealignment where the electorate no longer vote along rigid class lines. The Independent reported in October 2018 that one of the most remarkable features of the 2017 general election was that Labour could no longer be described as a predominantly working-class party. In the 2017 election there was hardly any class difference between Labour and Conservative voters.

This is significant as it shows while historically class was an important determiner of voting behaviour, this is no longer the case, perhaps because people do not identify so closely with social class as they used to.

Ipsos MORI found that in the 2017 general election, the middle classes swung to Labour, while working classes swung to the Conservatives. Although the Conservatives maintained a six-point lead among ABC1s, Labour increased its vote share among this group by 12 points since 2015.

This is significant as it supports the view that the electorate are no longer motivated by class alignment and traditional expectations that middle classes will vote for more right-wing political parties with the working classes more likely to vote for left-wing political parties.

A survey published by BMG Research in 2018, found that in 2017, instead of class identity, identities based on values are "highly predictive" of how people vote. The electorate may make a decision to vote for a particular party based on single issues, such as the ban on fox hunting or Tim Farron's views on same-sex relationships. This is important as it shows that people may not be driven by class but by issues that transcend income levels or employment status.

This would mean that today people are more motivated by their social, economic or religious values than by class alignment.

When we consider that in 2014, YouGov asked people whether they regarded themselves as "working class", "middle class" or "upper class", nine million ABC1 adults said that they considered themselves to be working class, while five million C2DE adults said that they were middle class. This is significant as it shows that people may not really understand the Ipsos MORI classification of people by employment status and therefore it becomes increasingly difficult to comment categorically that class has a tangible role to play in measuring voting behaviour. When political researchers use one classification model to measure voting behaviour and the electorate another driven perhaps by aspiration or income level, it is almost impossible to determine the true impact that class has on voting behaviour.

The term 'class' is emotive and riven with ideals that it has taken on a meaning that only really pertains to the individual and therefore is not truly measurable.

YouGov claims that "the class divide in British politics seems to have closed and it is no longer a very good indicator of voting intention". It seems that the electorate no longer identifies itself so strongly with class as it did pre-1980s. John Curtice, professor of politics at Strathclyde University, claimed that the reason why people no longer identify so strongly with class is that in order to achieve election success, political parties need to appeal to a broad demographic rather than pitting its hopes on one section of society.

Curtice commented that "It's perfectly obvious why the Labour Party should have wanted to change its class image because the one thing that has undoubtedly has changed about class in Britain is the size of the classes...and the working class, which is traditionally associated with the Labour vote, has become the smaller of the classes".

This is significant as it shows that political parties need to ensure that their message touches a wide range of voters and is relatively centrist so as to appeal to the majority of the electorate. If people vote along single issue lines before their class, it seems obvious that political parties must adapt their message to suit. Therefore, while historically the Conservative Party would have targeted their low-income tax policies towards the wealthy and Labour would have simply focused on the rights of workers, political pragmatism means that this is no longer the case.

Ipsos MORI reported that in the EU Referendum of 2016, age and class both had an effect on voting behaviour. A majority of 18-34 year olds in every social class voted to remain, while a majority of those aged 55+ in every class voted to leave. But within each age group the middle-classes were more likely to vote to remain, and the working classes more likely to vote to leave, and within each class younger people were more likely to vote remain, and older people more likely to vote to leave. The crossover point was among the middle-aged: middle-class 35-54 year olds voted to stay, working class 35-54 year olds voted to leave.

This is significant as it shows a direct correlation between age and class in relation to the Brexit vote. It would seem that among younger people of all classes, 'remain' was the favoured option, whereas for older people of all classes, leave was favoured. That said, it would seem that there was overwhelming support for remain among middle classes while the working classes voted to leave. This shows that there is a direct link between class and voting behaviour within the 2016 Referendum.

Evaluation

Overall, it would be fair to evaluate that identifying what really drives voting behaviour is complex. It would seem that when people vote they are motivated by multiple factors which may relate to their age, the newspapers they read, social media accounts that they follow, television programmes that they watch and their perception of their social class.

It is fair to suggest that all of these factors can impact the decision that people make, however, other factors such as gender, the importance of single issues (such as the environment, Brexit or transgender issues, for example), geographical location and ethnicity may also play a significant role. We must not categorise individuals as homogenous groups – not all young or old people vote in the same way and not all Guardian readers vote Labour. We must also consider the issue of the self-categorisation of social class.

While Ipsos MORI offers social grade classifications, some people will identify with an alternative class based on their aspirations or definitions of class. It could also be the case that individuals are motivated by a group dynamic and may vote along familial lines. In addition, individuals could vote strategically, not voting for their political party of choice, but instead voting for a party that will keep out a party that they dislike and has more chance of winning an election.

Ways in which citizens can influence government decision-making.

Pressure groups play an important role in influencing government decision-making. Pressure groups are not political, but instead driven by an interest in a single issue or represent a group of people with a shared interest, career or issue. There are thousands of pressure groups in the UK today that aim to influence the government through lobbying, protesting or by providing expert knowledge about particular issues.

Insider groups

Some groups are described as 'insider' pressure groups and these enjoy the attention of the government - their views and opinions are valued by ministers and they are often consulted by the government and their recommendations often form the basis of government policies. Examples of insider pressure groups include the British Medical Association (BMA) and the National Farmers' Union (NFU).

CASE STUDY: The British Medical Association

The BMA works to represent doctors both individually and collectively, working with UK governments to lobby for improvements to health and health care. In August 2018, the BMA, working in equal partnership with NHS Employers and the Department of Health and Social Care (DHSC) began the review of the 2016 junior doctor contract in England.

The BMA has focused on resolving issues raised by its members, including tackling fatigue, improving rostering, and securing improvements for less than full time trainees. The pressure group were able to secure commitments from the government to review safety and training and ensuring that junior doctors do not miss out on training, or work excessive hours, because of service pressures. The BMA has also played an integral role in the current gender pay gap review process gender pay gap in medicine that is being carried out by the Department of Health and Social Care group.

The pressure group has highlighted issues such as women being under-represented in senior jobs, the unequal impact of parenting responsibilities and part-time work. This shows that insider pressure groups can play an integral role in influencing government decision-making as without this pressure from medical professionals, it may be the case that the government would not have tackled issues such as the junior doctor scandal that came to light in 2016 in conjunction with huge media coverage.

Discussing these issues with the government can avoid the possibility of strike action from medical professionals which would have a detrimental impact on public health. By presenting a collective voice from the medical professionals, the majority of which work for the government-run NHS, the BMA wield a significant amount of influence as the government need to listen to them in order to safeguard the smooth operation of the NHS.

In March 2020, during the Covid-19 pandemic, Dr Chaand Nagpaul, head of the British Medical Association, said the priority of the NHS needed to be the testing of doctors. The BMA also lobbied the government for ensure sufficient PPE supplies. The BMA stated that if doctors were to treat patients effectively during the COVID-19 crisis, then they must be protected from the virus as they carried out their duties.

Furthermore, the BMA are committed to investigating the alarming statistics indicating the greater impact of the virus on BAME (black, Asian and minority ethnic) healthcare workers and the wider community. The BMA claim that it is vital that there is greater understanding of the issues and the underlying factors as well as the proper support in place for BAME healthcare and other public sectors workers.

In order to draw attention to this issue and demand action, the BMA was the first major body to call for - and secure - a national inquiry into the disproportionate of COVID-19 on BAME healthcare workers and communities. The group also lobbied for and secured a risk assessment framework to ensure that vulnerable and BAME doctors who are at highest risk of death from COVID-19 are better protected.

A roundtable discussion was hosted by the BMA following the release of the Public Health England review of the issue in early June with 13 leading BAME medical groups.

The BMA has become a leading voice on BAME issues with its chair of council discussing this topic on all main news outlets – across the main broadcast outlets as well as national and regional media.

BMA representatives were invited to meet and discuss the issue with officials from Number 10, government ministers, leader of the opposition, and senior officials across PHE and NHS England.

In addition, BMA representatives were engaged in public webinars to raise the profile of the issue.

The BMA has been instrumental in highlighting the plight of many doctors on the front line during the pandemic. The BMA is a powerful organisation. It aims to safeguard the rights of its members and can call for strike action should health workers be placed in unsafe working conditions in terms of a lack of equipment, the experience of vulnerable groups of workers or working hours.

This does mean that groups like the BMA can derail public healthcare provision if their members withhold their medical services and expertise. In some respects, the government cannot afford to ignore or dismiss the views and opinions of the BMA and therefore this group's influence is far-reaching.

CASE STUDY: The National Farmers' Union

The NFU claims that it is the most successful representation body for agriculture and horticulture in England and Wales. This insider pressure group gives a voice and protection of the lives of agricultural workers now and in the future. Its purpose is to champion British agriculture and horticulture, to campaign for a stable and sustainable future for British farmers and to secure the best possible deal for its members. In 2018 the NFU focused on simultaneously lobbying for police services and Government to tackle rural crime while advancing the best interests of British farming in the Brexit discussions. The NFU works to influence government decision-making through its Government and Parliamentary Affairs operation which represents and promotes the views of the NFU in London to a wide range of stakeholders, by monitoring political developments which affect the farming and growing industries, by influencing the political agenda through meetings, briefings and legislative amendments and lobbying Parliament in line with the NFU's communications strategy.

In recent years the NFU lobbied successfully for an exemption from the ban on treating flowering crops with neonicotinoid pesticides, which are nerve agents that have been shown to cause a harm to honeybees and wild bees.

Critics of the NFU and these pesticides were dismayed by this result considering the impact to the bee population which is integral to the pollination of crops. However, this shows the considerable political influence of some insider groups, such as the NFU. The NFU as an insider group is part of the consultation process enables them to use direct methods in order to exert influence on government decision-making.

A survey conducted by OnePoll in July 2020 revealed that 75% of Britons have a positive view of the farming industry – the highest figure since the Farmer Favourability Survey began in 2012. This news came out around the same time that the UK government would be debating a proposed Trade Bill covering the UK'S post-Brexit trade deals.

The farming industry is worth around £120 billion, and supporters are keen to protect it. The NFU sent a petition to the government signed by more than a million people to ensure that future agreements do not lead to food imports that would be illegal to produce here, such as chlorinated chicken or hormone-fed beef.

The farming industry, which employs more than four million people in the UK, is regarded by 89% of the public as being 'fairly or very important' to the economy. It is perhaps this sense of social and economic importance that ensures that the NFU are well supported particularly on its petition. Furthermore, more than 78,000 people also wrote to their MP urging them to support the introduction of a Trade, Food and Farming Standards Commission that can review trade policy and develop solutions that can hold all food imports to the UK's high standards.

NFU president Minette Batters said: "It has been overwhelming to see this volume of support. The fact that more than one million people have signed a petition urging the government to put into law rules that prevent food being imported to the UK which is produced in ways that would be illegal here is a clear signal of how passionate the British public feel about this issue."

Outsider groups

Some pressure groups can be described as 'outsider groups' as they do not enjoy the advantages of 'insider groups'.

Outsider groups are not consulted or called upon by government ministers and they are not consulted during the policy-making process. As a result, some outsider groups have to use different strategies to gain attention for their cause.

CASE STUDY: Fathers 4 Justice

One example of an outsider pressure group is Fathers 4 Justice. This is a fathers' rights organisation that aims to gain public and parliamentary support for changes in UK legislation on fathers' rights. It has campaigned for equal rights for fathers following a separation from their partners.

The group has been involved in a number of high-profile protests to publicise their cause. These have included two men throwing packages of flour dyed purple at Tony Blair during prime minister's questions in May 2004, a man dressed as Spiderman scaling the London Eye and staging an 18-hour protest that closed the attraction in September 2004, a campaigner dressed as Batman staging a five-hour protest on a ledge by the Buckingham Palace balcony, one man defaced a painting of the Queen in Westminster Abbey and finally a plot by fringe members to kidnap Tony Blair's son. For some, the group is one to ridicule rather than to take seriously, however their high profile actions that have been broadcast and written about in the mainstream media has helped to keep the issue of paternity rights in the public eye. The group would argue that such actions, legal and illegal, have been more effective than negotiations with the political and legal establishment.

Access rights for separated fathers have improved significantly in the last decade, with one major change being the introduction of new shared parenting laws introduced in 2012 which seeks to ensure that fathers are given the legal right to spend time to develop a meaningful relationship with their sons or daughters. This is important as it could be argued that the actions of F4J has promoted discussion, debate and mobilised public opinion on key issues which has in turn been picked up by the media which has helped to influence government decision-making.

In April 2019, F4J activists staged a protest at Madame Tussauds over the plight of 1 million Grandparents denied access to their Grandchildren. The timing of this was crucial as Prince Harry and Meghan Markle were about to have their first child. The F4J supporters hoped to harness the publicity surrounding the issue of whether Meghan Markle's father (Thomas Markle) would be allowed to see his grandchild as he is estranged from his daughter.

The activists wore Thomas Markle masks and attached stickers to waxworks of the Royal couple that read "GrandFathers4Justice". They then taped themselves to the dummies using "fragile" tape. This shows that F4J have gained publicity for their cause by using the media and prominent locations in order to harness media coverage. However, this publicity has been largely negative and the political aims of the group which include greater transparency in family courts, are as yet unachieved.

CASE STUDY: Stonewall

Stonewall is an outsider pressure group committed to supporting and protecting the rights of the LGBT community. The groups states that its mission is to "ensure that laws and rights essential for LGBT equality are created, maintained, protected and defended, so that LGBT people have equal rights here and abroad."

The group uses various methods to enact change, such as lobbying governments to change laws that do not ensure equality for LGBT people, or laws that do not go far enough. Stonewall mounted a successful campaign which resulted in Parliament passing the Civil Partnerships Act in 2004 and legalising gay marriage (Same Sex Couples Act) 2013.

In addition, this pressure group has achieved major successes including helping achieve the equalisation of the age of consent, lifting the ban on LGB people serving in the military, securing legislation which allowed same-sex couples to adopt. This shows how an outsider group can make effective use of lobbying to encourage and achieve progressive legislative change and ensure equality for all groups irrespective of their gender identification or sexual orientation.

Evaluation

It could be argued that pressure groups play an important role in influencing government decision-making.

All types of pressure group help to highlight issues that may be too sensitive or emotive for government to consider tackling.

In addition, pressure groups are an essential part of the democratic process as they allow citizens to express viewpoints at any point, without having to wait for a general election or referendum to express their political views. Pressure groups represent minority groups or local issues and help to encourage diversity and representation. Insider groups can offer expertise and help to influence government policy, however outside groups can struggle to gain traction for their cause as they are not included in the inner workings of government.

This makes insider groups more effective and impactful than outsider groups. As a result of outsider groups feeling on the fringe of political influence, they can often resort to dramatic publicity stunts to gain attention for their cause. It can also be the case that some outsider groups will resort to illegal activities to gain publicity and this can result in negative press for their cause as the group appears irrational and criminal in its approach.

This can be incredibly damaging for a pressure group and result in it being frozen out of the mainstream press and serious political or public debate. The influence of the media cannot be overstated. It is certainly the case that celebrity endorsement and media interest can help to propel a cause of a pressure group and make it a 'political hot potato' that will attract newspaper column inches and television interviews. Lobbying MPs can be highly effective for all types of pressure groups and as such this tactic is favoured by many groups seeking change or influence in the political arena.

Ultimately, the success of a pressure group in achieving its aims through influencing government decision-making depends on the cohesion of individual group, funding, membership numbers, media attention, the political party in power, and the time period in which the group are operating.

About the author

Hannah Young has worked as a secondary school teacher for 17 years teaching History, Politics, Modern Studies and Philosophy.

Other titles by this author:

- Social Inequalities in the UK: Higher Modern Studies Course Notes (2020)

  ISBN-13: 978-1792923388

- International Terrorism: Higher Modern Studies Course Notes (2020)

  ISBN-13: 979-8663198028

Printed in Great Britain
by Amazon